BOYS, GIRLS

Boys, Girls represents poetry that grapples with the subconscious battle of reality and imagination. The words ask to be read slowly, with grief and a warm cup of tea.

Copyright © 2013 Kevin Gunn, Odette Metamorph, Nicole Pomeroy, Cesar Reyes, Michelle Tran

All Rights Reserved.

ISBN: 0615775977
ISBN-13: 9780615775975

Boys, Girls

ACKNOWLEDGMENTS

California poets Kevin Gunn, Odette Metamorph, Nicole Pomeroy, Cesar Reyes, and Michelle Tran want to thank the tragedies, interiorities and the fine lines between sanity and going over the edge for the push into writing words worth reading.

Gunn, Metamorph, Pomeroy, Reyes, Tran

Contents

Kevin Gunn   1
   A Steady Wind
   Seams
   Workbench
   Speaking in Tongues

Odette Metamorph   7
   Recollection of Self
   Hands Cupped

Nicole Pomeroy   9
   The Reading Nook
   A Head Full of Salt and Black Sands
   Walking Anachronism
   Histrionics
   Untitled
   Crass Manipulation

Cesar Reyes   15
   Coffee
   Warmth
   Words
   Berkeley
   Whitman
   Insecurity

Michelle Tran   21
   Defilement
   Beautiful Awakening
   Standing on the Ledge
   The Lilies

KEVIN GUNN

A Steady Wind

Father and son eat breakfast at a diner in a glass silence:
"I'm sorry son, people fall out of love."

Time has spread the family, rearranged beds,
sanded down the perfect pieces of their jigsaw puzzle.
The four pieces that once, fit fondly together on a couch
glazed by the lights of a Christmas tree.

Seams

"Ikit" is the Igorot word for grandfather,
mine was a proud man.

He wore horn-rim glasses, with one lens pushed out
because his right eye was still good.
In the Philippines, the school boys would stand on opposite
sides of a dry creek bed and throw rocks at one another,
a man was not supposed to flinch.
My grandfather did not flinch.

As a rambunctious, often reckless little boy,
when I broke things he would ask me if I wanted to build
great things or break them:
In the question there was one answer.

"There is nothing we cannot fix,
though, the seems may betray us."

1942, Bontoc, Philippines: my grandpa sits in a blue Buick,
watches his father argue with a Japanese solider at the
gate of the All Saints Mission,now a ramshackle prison with
tall fences of iron toothed wire.
His father has been caught smuggling letters
 in the seams of his suit to the men inside.
He is shot in front of my grandfather.

1972: President Marcos declares martial law.
My grandfather packs up his family and flees.
He will get a job as a gas station attendant,
the great business tycoon will wash toilets the rest of his life.

2003: I will graduate from junior high;
my grandfather lies in a hospital bed in the back room
of the house I grew up in.
The cancer has eaten him—

left black marks across his collarbones.
His chest crackles like crumpled leaves.

He died screaming, and I held his hand.
His favorite little grandson.
His clumsy little builder.

Years later, I seek to sugar the daggers of memory,
I'll remember an evening
We sat on the couch watching television,
I turned to him in the blue light
his face is wet, he is staring 3,000 miles away at the home
he left on a hill in the Philippines.

Without blinking, never losing sight of that now vacant
place, he said to me:

"There's a divinity that shapes our ends,
rough-hew them how we will.
 Though, I've lost more than I could ever have won,
I promise, there's nothing we cannot fix,
though the seems may betray us."

Workbench

Will you make another son?
I'll be busy behind, cleaning up your mess.
Can't I be close to you?
Or is it my fault too,
didn't I do well enough at school?
Look, I've made something of me.
You, who taught me how to ride,
how to fix fences and to write.
How dare you leave this house you built,
and this family, with it you filled.
Can't I be close to you?

Speaking in Tongues

I sit cross legged on the white linoleum floor in a fast growing pool of blood. The artery in my thigh gapes a red maw, I planned to end my life. I've jammed a pair of fingers into my groin to retard the flow of crimson. It hurts and I've bled enough that I feel out of focus, like the edges of me have become frayed in the effort of staying together. I know I need to keep my hands here—I am just so surprised at the pain.

The hum of the garage door purrs. The little growl dances on the membrane of my ear: salvation. "Mother," I try shouting; instead a slurry whine. I keep trying. My chest cycles like an unbalanced piston.

I pause to listen, nothing—then, a rapid report of hard foot falls on the stairs. She's calling my name. I'm suddenly ashamed of what she's about to see. Her adult-sized son sitting in the bathroom wearing nothing but a pair briefs: ruining her new tile.

I paw at the towels on the rack above me. One shakes loose and drag it over my stomach and crotch. It's difficult to keep pressure on my thigh. She comes through the door and for a moment she wears a plain unbelieving mask, like a child struck for the first time. She doesn't speak— just starts to cry. As the tears make swirling black rivulets of her mascara, she looks so small in her uniform. I can't believe that I grew out of her. Her scrubs are faded green, a few sizes too big, like drooping sails, billowy around her petite frame. I start the slow drift onto the sea of sleep.

~~~

My mother never said a hurtful word when I came home from college that December. She just pulled the duffel bag off my shoulder with a solemn nod and carried it inside. She was so kind, pretending not to see me crying on the back porch, sucking down cigarettes, shaking bruised knuckles at the winter air.

I came to live on her couch. Each day, I heard the front

door open and I could feel her looking at me in a long pause before it slams shut. I almost can hear her thinking, asking, what she did do to
deserve such a thing.

~~~

I am on couch in Dr. Phelman's office. I can see he wants to reach out and touch my hands. "I can see today you're feeling especially raw. Why don't we take advantage of that and probe into how you were feeling when you had your—accident?"

I remember looking at him for a long while, tasting the film of my teeth. "You know? Almost every night: I fill the tub with warm water, almost to the brim. I submerge everything but my nose, hearing nothing but the sterile buzz of silence. Then the water goes still. That must be what death is. A sweet nothing."

Odette Metamorph

Recollection of the Self

Shadows rest under my eyes
and the grief of death falls in the pits
of crow's feet at the corners,
Permanent black lines carved in my skin
from muddled tears and the silence
of my own death whispering in my ears.
Childless and free I had no grasp--
I controlled the chains tightened at my ankles
and barbed wire cutting into my breasts,
restrained with a ball gag and the deprecation
I granted to the internal rhyme scheme,
the voices that refuse to quiet my innards
as they are sliced with the edge of a rose petal.

Hands Cupped

When you sip a mug
of sugary chocolate, I sink
into my compostable mug of black
coffee no sugar.
Black brown eyes peering up at me,
I smile.
I laugh.
I say don't bother.
I'll stand,
waiting for you to tell me to sit down already,
I walk with you and my hands shake,
I have more to say--
Nearly years have passed between the moment
my heart settled on you that I could stand
the notion of being with—
As you sip warmth, cradle the cup,
I just want to hold your hand.

Boys, Girls

Nicole Pomeroy

The Reading Nook

His lips were often left
just a millimeter or two unlatched
as he thumbed through pages
of Hollinghurst, or Wilde,
    or sometimes Whitman,
his voice always trailing off.
as he read passages out loud

He inhales the distinct, stagnant air,
deeply, cautiously,
the kind of air that exists only in worn college bedrooms,
and looks at her.

She was burrowed in a nest of blankets,
dreaming of the smell of rain on asphalt,
of cold currents streaming through her body,
quivering and electric.

A Head Full of Salt and Black Sands

I have opened my mind to discover
    that it has gone missing.
perhaps sinking into swamps filled with
    corpses and porcelain,
While I stay still in a decaying rocking chair
whose legs have been replaced by fishtails, dried and brittle
like homes of savages, left defenseless in heaven's sour cold.
    I felt it dive into the ocean
where I found the city once built in my dreams,
    I used to be my own creator of everything.

Walking Anachronism

A twenty-first century diagnosis of hysteria
locked me in a lighthouse
with an inkwell
and an ocean
and the humming of whales to lull me to sleep.

I carve out the stomachs of sea urchins
to find pearls,
sticky and rough,
their effervescence depleted
after being ripped from their mothers womb

I take them home with me,
build nets of broken shells and colored sands
and wake to open-mouthed oysters,
their tongues wrapped around my limbs,
as I'm trawled from the tangled net of blankets
and thrown into the sea.

Histrionics

The yellowed leaves are left
wet with imprints from a head full of decaying teeth
you've digested all you can bear,
left satiated, groaning
clawing at floorboards ripe with echoes of
hungry breaths.

I'm left with the stories of gravediggers,
the body memory preservers.
They smoke cigarettes,
leaving muddy footprints in the hallway closet
where they sleep,
listening to the docile tapping of drizzle on cement,
it was a rhythm only known
to faces etched with anxious contours
and secrets hidden in thickets of bone marrow.

I tell them I want to know
what it's like to bury bodies, teeming with pasts,
deep underground, never to be resurfaced
(except for in nightmares,
and maybe horror movies).

I tell them I want to know
because we don't talk about
our histories anymore.

Untitled

The fallacy of tongues ridden with lust
The one that could trace the curves of her neck
In such a way
That every bone in her body would
Exhale
The mouthful of soot, of smoke
Bellies heaving
In a bed of liquored gems and ash

The taste of wax melting

Crass Manipulation

I always imagined his voice in my head,
the drab, frayed cadences,
enormous in the damp air.

I'd heard his labored breaths from where I stood,
cascading toward the door,
I wanted to believe I could hear his bones
      Collapse
each joint cold and cracking,
hiding beneath a cosmic array of skin,
the daunting, foul frontier
of huntsmen in the east.

I looked through him, hard
I hated him with that gaze,
and I knew he felt it.

Cesar Reyes

Coffee

She looks at me
with lips quivering.
A softness reflected
by her brown hair.
I wonder what lies
unspoken behind her
white teeth
and the deepness
of her stare.

Warmth

On a cold night
in a small town all too familiar
our breathe touches lightly
in the darkness;
teeth chattering in anticipation.
she cups her hands to her lips,
releasing a hot sigh,
as I sip on a keystone light;
fingers slowly wiping the excess.
Her pelvis leans, deep forward,
Back cool lying against the wall.
As if occupying mouths
could ever stop
the inevitable.

Words

She says:
"I can't hear you, I
can only hear myself"
with the hair dryer on,
close to her ear.

Berkeley

we sit on a patch of grass
(what downtown Berkeley likes
to call a park)
with A's dog, Ahji,
who smells used syringes.
J sits next to me twiddling thumbs
as buildings hover over;
listening intently.
She tells stories of threesomes
and drunken nights at bars with
men who have no names.
I tell her it's good she's having fun.
She tells me she misses home.

Whitman

I can hear a pounding in a head
Not too far from me.
She sits crossed legged on a table over
Echoing chants of success and
Fears of failure through a cell phone
That dangles a hello kitty key chain.
How are we of the same mind?
You and i.

Insecurity

I wonder how she looks
at me
when I'm not around.
how her mind
frames Me,
what looking back
does for Her
when she sits silently
on sunday mornings
drinking coffee.

I wonder if she spreads a light smile
and its good as the jam
on her toast.

but I wonder more,
on cloudy days when distance
takes its grasp,
if there's another to keep her warm.

Michelle Tran

Defilement

You chip away at me,
hoping to sculpt a masterpiece,
you scrape away my dreams
filling my cracks and seams,
with your artistic vision.

You mold me until it hurts.
Pushing and pulling,
bending and breaking,
twisting and tearing,

Rubbing raw my skin
with your ruthless words

Til I am polished to your liking.

Alcohol-
Removes-
     my shellac skirt.

Your white paint-
Forced-
     on a collectible piece.

After.

The fragments of your
scrap pile.

Beautiful Awakening

She mocks me in all of my attempts,
and yet she urges me on.
Until I'm tired-
Until I'm starved-
Until there is nothing left of me.

She takes everything away,
With intentions to cure, but only harms.
Now, I am growing faint-
on this path of self-destruction,
on this road of isolation.

She rules me by numbers,
as I ignore the hunger…
for beauty and perfection,
to the extent of desperation.

To be weightless and fragile-
even if it is my own private exile.

To be lovely and finally free,
Oh, she begs for the "ideal" me.

Standing on a Ledge

Standing on a ledge,
No one can touch me.
No one can hurt me.
No one can fill my heart with lies,
or make me endure broken promises.

Escape is given here-
Standing on a ledge.

Where I am between the heavens,
and the all-consuming reality.

All is still.
All is in motion.

Touched by the invisible wind.
Kissed by the shining sun.
My mind becomes undone…

Standing on a ledge-
I am stripped of it.
The pressure becomes weightless.

No more expectations.
No more facades.

Standing on a ledge.
Where all is bare.
Where all is beautiful.

The Lilies

You plucked each petal,
and bruised each stem.
You wanted each and every one of them.
The sepals were torn off,
and thrown in disarray.
Their blooms misshaped,
and scattered away.

Five pink lilies, sisters of spring.
The flowers left wilted,
No joy could they bring.
Oh, the horror on everyone's face!
Found near their mother, the shattered vase.

Dripping onto their carpet,
their perfume left a stain.
Life without the Lilies—
Which culprit to blame?

Solace

The fairy tales have burned.
Ashes scattered across the sea.
The soot smeared on my cheek,
a small shade of my identity.
Like tears of ink upon paper,
bounded and abandoned into books,
never read nor ever heard
yet always seemingly overlooked.

Hush

My blood cascades beneath
my skin—hush, as the candles flicker.
Oh, it draws you in.
Shadows on our bare—

But *your blood* replies, shallow breath,
touching—
my velvety, skin—it whispers, hush.

The flame licks the cherry blossom lips.
Its taste and fragrance—a head rush.
Hush.

Pleasure with your eyes, painting
slow, long, and deep—
The wave, upon wave,
my cries.
You tell me teasingly,
hush.

Consuming *our shared blood*
a fire breathes.
Burning the roots of the family tree.

It's
Over.
The
End.
Of
Poetry
Today.
Read
More.

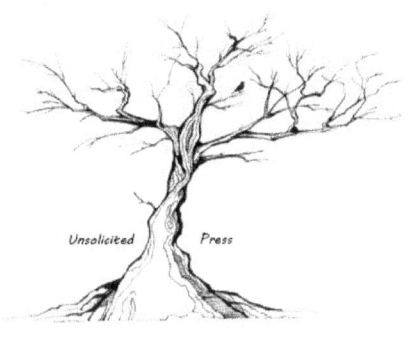

www.ingramcontent.com/pod-product-compliance
Lightning Source LLC
Chambersburg PA
CBHW031439040426
42444CB00006B/889